A Blueprint for a Modern Society

Redesigning Democracy, Novel Solutions for Consolidation of Power in Government, Fair Taxation, Election Fraud, Immigration, and Equitable Access to the Law.

Rob Pendell

ISBN 978-1-63784-635-3 (paperback)
ISBN 978-1-63784-636-0 (digital)

Hawes & Jenkins Publishing
16427 N Scottsdale Road Suite 410
Scottsdale, AZ 85254
www.hawesjenkins.com

Printed in the United States of America

Contents

Introduction

Human society is amazingly complex. It represents, by far, the most complex social structure on the planet. No other organism operates in a cooperative manner that is even close to the complexity of human society. Beehives may have up to 60,000 bees per hive, and an ant colony may have up to half a million ants. Although these are certainly examples of large-scale organizational structures in nature, there seems to be very little evidence that there are any individual relationships happening within these organizations. On the other hand, if we look at other cooperative pack animals like wolves, dolphins, orcas, primates, and others, where there is definitely evidence of not only cooperative behavior but also deep individual relationships, the groups never grow larger than fifty to seventy-five individuals before splitting into separate groups. In 2023, the US military numbered 1.4 million soldiers.[1] Organized into numerous commands; divided into brigades, divisions, fleets, flights, squads, and teams of all sorts and sizes; all operating under numerous commanders, generals, admirals, etc.; all under the command of one department under the command of one individual; and all working toward one large objective and many smaller objectives in relative harmony. All while each individual maintains numerous personal and intimate relationships, both friendly and unfriendly. It is an amazing thing. Now include

---

[1]   https://www.google.com/search "How many soldiers in the US military"

all other types of organizations—governmental, religious, familial, public, and private—represented in human society. It's easy to see that the complexity of human society is unmatched, at least on this planet.

How do we do it? What keeps us from just killing each other in a mad rush for survival or the acquisition of resources? We do seem to do that rather well too.

There have been volumes, and even whole schools, dedicated to the study of this very question. Throughout history, many systems have been utilized to keep the organizational complexities of human societies operating smoothly. Human society has grown and evolved from cave dwellers to hunting and gathering nomads, domesticated animal husbands, simple farmers, then village dwellers, machine users, cities, and countries. Each stage of human societal evolution had its own way of managing the people in it and the society's activities for survival.

The human race is well into an unprecedented new stage of human and societal evolution—the information age. Never before in the history of the human race have we had so much access to information and each other. With this new closeness, new problems that, just a decade ago, could be easily ignored, overlooked, or marginalized through isolation have now become a part of everyone's daily reality. The growth and development of AI, which increases our ability to process vast amounts of data beyond our imagination, may possibly create new ways of thinking about nearly everything.

This is an amazing opportunity for humans to reach new, unimagined potential.

The "horseless carriage" has evolved into the Tesla˚. Both cars do essentially the same thing, in essentially the same way. But one is wildly more complex and has capabilities that couldn't even be conceived of by the other. Just like the horseless carriage, the governing systems and societal organizations have evolved to accommodate the changing demands and complexities of an ever-changing human society. A 1990 Toyota is a huge step forward from the horseless carriage. We need to begin to evolve how we think and organize our society to the Tesla˚ of societal organization.

This evolution will require some fundamental changes in how we think about society as a whole, our place and role in society, and how we relate to each other. Some of these changes may be difficult. Change is hard. I get it. Our founding fathers knew this. So much so, they took the time to actually put it into the Declaration of Independence.

> …Prudence, indeed, will dictate that Governments long established should not be changed for light and transient causes; and accordingly all experience hath shewn, that mankind are more disposed to suffer, while evils are sufferable, than to right themselves by abolishing the forms to which they are accustomed… [2]

Our founding fathers had the benefit of great separation from the system they were trying to change; we do not. Those in power will resist it, as it will change the nature and structure of power. And, as we all know, the only thing powerful people fear is losing their power.

As Niccolo Machiavelli wrote in his famous book *The Prince*:

> It aught to be remembered that there is nothing more difficult to take in hand, or more perilous to conduct, or more uncertain in its success, than to take the lead in the introduction of a new order of things. Because, the innovator has for enemies all those who have done well under the old conditions, and lukewarm defenders in those who may do well under the new.

Therefore, I put forward this theoretical treatise to the world as a novel form of societal organization. It is based on the perspective of an American citizen living within the United States in the early

---

[2]   Unites States Declaration of Independence, Chpt 2.

part of the twenty-first century, observations from the first experiment conducted by our founding fathers, the results of those policies after 250 years, and cursory observations of other systems around the world—both current and historical. This is not an attempt to undermine or overthrow any established government, but a series of ideas for anyone involved in the evolutionary process of society.

Make no mistake. I have no illusions about the chances that these changes will replace the deeply entrenched and established system anytime soon. Change takes time.

An Unpleasant Truth

Humans aren't perfect. It's been said that humans are a flawed species.

We all struggle with a mixture of basic animal desires, intellectual ideals, emotions, spiritual or divine inspiration and beliefs, and perceptions tainted by a lifetime of conditioning by the media, family, community, religion, trauma, abuse, addiction, self-interest, and a myriad of other things that cause us to see things the way we do. These things cannot be changed.

If we take a really objective look at ourselves, I think it will be fair to assume that everyone operates out of some form of motivated self-interest. Why wouldn't we? Survival, after all, is hardwired into us all. It's one of the most basic principles of all life, humans included. I believe it's fair to say that everyone will, at least, consider doing for themselves before doing for others. Even purely altruistic actions often come from a desire, conscience or not, to feel good about oneself.

How each individual resolves this consideration to do for themselves on an instant-to-instant basis is impossible to predict, but I believe it's fair to say that everyone considers it before all other considerations.

All of us are constantly dealing with temptations and weaknesses in our minds and spirits. Each of us must deal with these in our own way as individuals. Oftentimes, we succumb to these weaknesses and temptations, often to the detriment of ourselves and those around us. These things are taken for granted as part of the human condition. We are what we are.

So in accepting this as an unchangeable part of the human condition, it would be wise for society to arrange itself in such a way to accommodate this, instead of, as we've done so often in the past, denying it by creating a set of ideal concepts that can never be achieved due to the simple and unchangeable nature of who we are. A perfect system cannot be created by imperfect people. There will always be those who will seek to pervert any system for their own purposes. Understanding and accepting this at the outset allows for systems to be put in place to limit, or at least hinder, the efforts of such people.

A Harmonious Society

Society is made up of three parts.

1. *Government* manages the logistics of society. It keeps the power and water on, insures the streets and highways are paved. It manages population density and expansion; provides fire and police protection and defense of the country, communities, and citizens; provides for commerce and trade through the development of some universally accepted currency; and does a myriad of other things required for society to run and grow smoothly.
2. *Industry* provides the products and services a society wants and needs, creates commerce, innovates, generates wealth and value, and produces the means for society to grow and prosper.
3. *The People* fill the myriad of positions in the other two and do the actual work. The People are the gears, cogs, bearings, nuts, and bolts of the giant societal machine. And just as in any machine, if those gears, cogs, and bearings aren't in their place and functioning, the machine begins to operate poorly or may actually just stop all together.

In the past, every large society has been organized in such a way that one of the three parts either rules over or attempts to rule over the other two—usually by force, coercion, or some other means of intimidation. Despotism, monarchy, autocracy, and theocracies are government-controlled. Capitalism, objectivism, and imperialism are industry-controlled. Democracy, communism, socialism, and republics are people-controlled. This, inevitably, leads to tension and discontentment among the ruled parts and often leads to internal strife.

A harmonious society is a single whole containing all three parts. No one part is more or less important than any other. All three must be working together in harmony, understanding their roles, and respecting the roles of the others. Each should be playing its part as needed, like a well-oiled machine or symphony. Imagine a cart full of cargo pulled by a horse. If we imagine society represented by this image, then the man driving the cart is government, the cart and its contents represent industry, and the horses represent the people. It requires all three to do their respective parts for it to work. If any piece steps out of its role, then the whole ceases to work properly. Society's view of itself should evolve into this perspective.

This, of course, will require a basic change in the way everyone thinks about society and their respective roles in it.

A Problem of Perspective

Our founding fathers, in their attempt to separate themselves from the oppressive autocratic rule of the king of England, penned into existence a statement to the world that put forth some fundamental ideas that have reshaped the world and how people everywhere view themselves.

For the first time in human history, the idea that a person's Rights were derived from the Creator and not from the state was put forth.[3] Using the basic concepts of Plato and the Roman Republic, our founding fathers attempted to create a new equitable form of national government. Concepts such as all men are created equal, separation of church and state, innocent until proven guilty, and others were novel concepts at the time. This grand experiment of a country governed by its people for its people was a brave and dangerous venture in the time of greedy kings and an oppressive church.

These men were highly educated, creative, and forward-thinking for their time. However, they were also subject to the limitations of the paradigms and cultural biases of the mid-1700s. It is impossi-

---

[3] The National Center for Constitutional Studies: The Unique Idea of the US Constitution. https://nccs.net/blogs/our-ageless-constitution/the-unique-idea-of-the-american-constitution.

ble for any modern person to relate to what life in the original colonies was like. The population of the entire country, all thirteen colonies, in 1776 was only 2.6 million.[4] There were fewer people than in many large cities today. There was no electricity, no running water, and no engines of any kind. If you imagine your image of the "old west" as portrayed in movies and such, that was nearly one hundred years after the time of the original colonies. Go twenty miles in any direction from the center of any colonial city in 1776, and you were in the wilderness, untouched by anyone other than the natives, who, at the time, were just as likely to kill you as anything else. It would take you all day to get there if you survived.

At the time, many people were slave owners and considered slavery perfectly acceptable, even their "God-given Right." Under the original Constitution, slavery was allowed and wasn't actually eliminated until nearly one hundred years later. Society as a whole primarily followed some form of Christian belief paradigm, with many being what we would currently refer to as fundamentalist, possibly even extremist. The concept of women's Rights was all but foreign to them. Anyone displaying homosexuality or gender issues was considered an abomination or degenerate and was often jailed or killed. Any person who wasn't "White" was generally considered a lesser being or savage. There was no science of human psychology. The understanding of large-scale management principles, mass production, and global communication was essentially nonexistent. The most basic things we simply take for granted today, in many cases, couldn't even be imagined by even the most forward-thinking individual. The Constitution was written by candlelight with a quill, not a pen, not even a pencil.

We can't chastise them for their beliefs or lack of knowledge, as these were just the societal mores and technical limitations of the time. Considering all of this, many of the founding fathers had taken great steps ahead of their peers in their thinking and awareness of many of these issues. But even the most forward-thinking of them could never, in their wildest dreams, conceive of an iPhone or the

---

[4] https://www.census.gov/library.

Internet and the effect it would have on our society, both locally and worldwide. Hell, we don't even fully understand it today. Not to mention the future possible effects of things like AI or fusion, two things we're currently on the verge of.

The founding fathers' ideas were both timely and world-changing. But today, they are simply inadequate for the demands of a society over two hundred times its size[5] with complexities unimaginable at the time.

That being said, these men set out to create the best form of government and society they could conceive. To that end, they sat down and wrote a Declaration of Independence to announce that, for very specific reasons, the thirteen colonies would no longer be subjected to the rule of a foreign king.

They then began the process of penning the parameters of their new government, the Constitution. My hat goes off to them for blazing the path that so many have followed. To date, over 190 countries have adopted a Constitutional form of government.[6] Though the structures of the governments themselves vary widely, most of them used our original document as a starting point for theirs.

The US Constitution was a grand experiment in governing, and over the years, many adjustments and changes (amendments) have had to be made to accommodate for lacks or omissions in the original document. These "patches" were fine at the time but now have become so numerous that the original, to this author, looks much like an old car held together with duct tape and bailing wire. Coupled with deviations from the original, such as executive orders, electoral college, restrictions on Rights for national security reasons, and others, I think it's fair to say that we've strayed from the path a bit.

---

[5]   Ibid.

[6]   www.constituteproject.org

Today, as we roll into the second quarter of the twenty-first century, our society struggles with numerous problems, as follows:

- An income gap so large that moving out of the lower levels of it seems next to impossible.
- Societal poverty is as high as it has ever been in this country and may compete with levels worldwide in some places.
- An educational standard that, in this author's opinion, is shameful for a first-world society.
- A dwindling middle class.
- There is no manufacturing base to speak of.
- Increasing inflation, rising costs of living, and low wages.
- Homelessness, addiction, and mental health issues in many of our major cities.
- An ideological divide of the likes, which may not have been seen since the Civil War.
- Automation is eliminating most of the basic and even some of the more complex manufacturing jobs.
- A government that is generally viewed as so corrupt and untrustworthy that nearly half the citizenry doesn't bother to participate in it, even in the simplest form—voting.

Now these issues are not specifically unique to our or any modern society. Every society must deal with these things and others, one way or another. But I think it would be safe to say they weren't high on the list of concerns for our founding fathers.

All People Have Value

Since there are as many perspectives as there are people, trying to get everyone to believe the same thing is useless. But giving everyone the feeling that who they are is important and that everyone, regardless of who they are, has a place in society can bring a universal sense of belonging and ownership. This feeling will naturally lead to a wider sense of care about our society as a whole.

This brings us to the first of the basic truths: "All people have value."

I believe our founding fathers tried to create this, but they were hindered by the paradigms and cultural restrictions of the time when they penned the Declaration of Independence.

> We hold these truths to be self-evident, that all
> men are created equal.

Unfortunately, it wasn't true then, isn't true now, and really never has been true. Now some argue that this statement refers to "in the eyes of God," and that indeed may be true, depending on which God you believe in. But in the eyes of our fellow man, it certainly is not. The reality of this may have greatly contributed to the disillusionment a great number of people in our society feel concerning the integrity of our government.

All Society Stratifies

Every single society, no matter how organized, no matter what governmental system is used, religious belief, or economic system utilized all the way back to bobo monkeys, has stratified. Every society is made up of essentially three levels, with some sublevels present occasionally. These are

- leaders,
- producers, and
- dependents.

This is normal and natural. Even the most basic tribal societies have their leaders, workers, and dependents. This stratification happens naturally due to variations in people's skill sets, competencies, abilities, family ties, ambitions, motivations, needs of society, luck, and a myriad of other things, including government control and the manipulation of powerful individuals. It happens in all societies.

By setting up the idea that all people have value in society as opposed to all people being equal in society, we create a truth that is easy to hold on to, regardless of your position in the stratification.

Your value is unique to yourself, while your equality must be compared to everyone else.

What we need to recognize is that, though we are not equal by any means, we do all have value, and that value must be respected. Is it all equal value? Of course not. Who's more valuable, the surgeon or the car wash boy? Well, one might say that the surgeon has more value, and in a medical emergency, one may be right. But at a car show or car dealership, where there is no medical emergency, the surgeon may not have any place at all. If the person who can make a fender shine like glass is in high demand, then who has the highest value?

Value is situational and therefore must be respected accordingly. Using the analogy of a car, which part has more value, the lug nuts or the steering wheel? It doesn't matter. Because without either, the car isn't going anywhere. It takes all the parts of a car doing what they're supposed to be doing. If any one part fails to do its job, the whole car is affected. Society is the same.

The highest-value thing is the one doing exactly what it was designed to do, exactly when it needs to be done. The rest of the time, its value may be less while other things are doing what they are designed to do. But it doesn't diminish the value of the first thing in the overall scheme. This is the idea we need to apply to everyone in society. Doing this is how we can approach a level of equality in society. It is, of course, impossible because everyone places a unique value on everything, but if we all recognize that each of us has a unique and specific value to society as a whole, then respect for each other's value will begin to improve our opinions of each other and, ultimately, how we treat each other.

Understand your own value in society. You are an important piece of a much larger machine, and without you and your value, society, as a whole, is diminished. This is an important point each person needs to come to within themselves. Creating a governmental and industrial system that approaches people and society with this precept in mind will begin to create a mindset population-wide. When people feel their parts are important and necessary, they will automatically perform their functions better.

Power

One definition of power is "the capacity or ability to direct or influence the behavior of others or the course of events."[7]

When considering power from a societal perspective, this is the definition we should concern ourselves with. One of the biggest threats to any society is too much power consolidated in one place for too long. There have been very few historical examples where someone, or a small group of people, obtained large amounts of societal power and then wielded that power with wisdom and benevolence for the benefit of society. Usually and all too often, once great societal power is obtained, that power corrupts those who've obtained it with delusions of grandeur, god complexes, or any number of other vices or corruptions, and the people and/or societies who find themselves under the control of this power suffer.

The quote "Power corrupts, and absolute power corrupts absolutely" is well-known. It was an observation that a person's sense of morality lessens as their power increases. There have certainly been many examples of its truth. Power is one of the most seductive temptations known, and many people have sacrificed much in its quest.

Societal power is only acquired in two ways: through political advancement and money. Typically, the combination of the two can create great problems if the individual or individuals in control of

---

[7] Oxford English Dictionary

that power and money are driven by self-interested motivations. It is generally the case, as anyone willing to accept the huge amount of work and sacrifice required to obtain those things is very motivated.

So it is wise for a society to put into place checks and balances to limit the consolidation of power in any one place for too long a time. The first place this must start is with the Law.

The Law

Because humans are humans. Because everyone, given the opportunity, will consider doing for themselves at the expense of others. Because, we as a species, cannot be trusted to make selfless or wise decisions for the benefit of the whole all the time. We have the Law.

Throughout history, the Law has attempted to reign over our more basic nature. In the very beginning, it was the simple Law of nature. Humans' dominance of the food chain was achieved through a pack-herd mentality. Our ability to work together for the benefit of the tribe allowed us to become the dominant species on the planet. Behavior contrary to the tribe's well-being was met with banishment from the protection and resources of the tribe. This was a virtual death sentence. Without the strength, protection, and resources of the tribe, an individual was or is at the mercy of nature, which is cruel and unforgiving.

A naked human, without fur, sharp teeth, or claws, is less suited to survival in nature than a newborn lamb. The lamb, at least, has a wool coat that will keep it from dying of exposure, at least until something eats it. A naked human, in most parts of the world, will die of simple exposure to the elements long before something eats it. Even if they managed to survive, without a tribe, they wouldn't prosper, grow, or thrive. A modern example of this is the popular television show *Naked and Afraid*. Most of the contestants are trained or experienced outdoorspeople, yet by the end of the challenge, many have had to drop out or be rescued. Those who complete the two-week challenge are almost always at their wit's end. Now this show always places the contestants in a warm climate. Conduct the show anywhere above or below the thirty-fifth parallel, and the show will be over in a number of days.

So by banishing individuals whose behaviors were contrary to the well-being of the tribe, the tribe submitted to the Law of nature. Those who acted contrary to the well-being of the tribe didn't survive. Banishment was so effective that the practice continued long after codified laws were established. Incarceration and imprisonment are simply evolved forms of banishment, though typically not as lethal.

As we evolved socially, the Law of nature was replaced by the Law of God. The Law of God dictates that behavior contrary to the well-being of society, as defined by God or his followers, will be punished by God and/or his followers. The result of which ended much in the same way as the tribal banishment—removal from the tribe or society and usually death—usually at the hands of God's followers.

As society continued to develop, the punishments became slowly less physically lethal and began to be more personal or spiritual in nature. Concern for your immortal soul is now at stake. The deeds of this life will be carried on into an eternity of reward or consequence in the next. This system of Law proved very effective. So much so that it is still in wide use to this very day in many modern societies. There was, or is, one fundamental flaw with it, though. That, of course, is humans.

Throughout history, God has chosen to only speak through individuals, who are then tasked with bringing the Word of God to the rest. Be it Moses, David, Jesus, Mohammad, Joseph Smith, or Jim and Tammy Baker, individuals speaking the Word of God abound. To my knowledge, I know of no instance where the heavens opened up and God spoke his Word to everyone, so everyone heard it and could understand it directly from the source. As a result, we, as a society, became reliant upon these messengers of God to interpret the Law of God for and to us.

Who's to say how many truly heard the voice of God, and how many saw an opportunity for some kind of advancement or power within society? How many were mentally ill and just heard voices in their heads? That question is unimportant.

What is important is that, eventually, from these individuals grew the church. Churches were designed to interpret and disseminate the Word and Law of God. I'm sure that the influence the church has had on human society and government is obvious to everyone. But as with all things involving humans, the church, in many cases, became corrupted by the failings of the humans within it. Greed, vanity, lust for power, and ambition drove individuals to increase the power and influence of the church to such an extent that even kings bowed before the church. The church got so powerful that it could, with a simple word, topple entire societies. Unfortunately, what happened was that the interpreters of God's Law—the priests, bishops, nuns, holy men, etc.—became immune to the Law. Who was there to hold them accountable? God? To speak out against the church or the actions of its representatives was considered heresy, and it was dealt with using the strongest measures. Being that these people were only humans, many were terribly corrupted by this power and immunity to question and committed gross atrocities in the name of God without consequence, at least in this life.

Our founding fathers, recognizing this, made another incredibly bold statement. In an attempt to keep the influence of the church out of the governing body of this new society, they penned a concept that literally condemned many of them to the threat of hanging. The First Amendment states: "Congress shall make no law respecting an establishment of religion, or prohibiting the free exercise thereof."

Thus as Thomas Jefferson wrote in a January 1, 1802, letter to the Danbury Baptist Association:

> I contemplate with sovereign reverence that act of the whole American people which declared that their legislature should, "make no law respecting an establishment of religion, or prohibiting the free exercise thereof," thus building a wall of separation between Church & State.

I believe what they were trying to accomplish here was to limit the ability of members of the church, to become "above the Law" as the saying goes. Having a clear separation between church and state presented the opportunity for the state to hold the church accountable for its actions. Essentially, it handed the rule of Law over to the state. This had the desired effect. The power and influence of the church have diminished substantially in the last 250 years in this country. Back to a position that, in this author's opinion, is where it rightfully should be—the personal, moral, and spiritual well-being of the individual.

Unfortunately, humans will be humans. The State is run by humans. So here we are, 250 years later, with a similar, if not identical, problem the founding fathers faced. Not that the members of the church find themselves above the Law, but now our lawmakers, law keepers, judges, lawyers, interpreters of the Law, and individuals within the State who've been elected to office by the People are now able to place themselves largely "above the Law." We are in a constant battle with "the powers that be" to hold these people accountable for their actions. Because those in power, like the church, interpret and enforce the Law, it's hard to find ways to prosecute those within the inner circle.

We're all humans. We're all endowed with a sense of self-interest and pack well-being. Very few of us will choose to prosecute ourselves for wrongdoing or those of us in our group. Thus we see that it has become exceedingly difficult to hold individuals within the legal system, at any level, accountable. From the senator to the local beat cop, this group or tribe of lawmakers or enforcers is a tribe of their own, and as such, they look out for and protect each other. Subsequently, we've seen some gross violations go unaccounted for because this group is hesitant to attack one of its own for fear that if one of them goes down, anyone of them can go down. Again, this brings us back to the nature of humans: self-interest and preservation through the protection of the tribe. As our founding fathers did with their revolutionary idea of separation of church and state. Another revolutionary idea's time has come—separation of Law and State.

Separation of Law and State

Arguably, the initial tool the church used in its attempt to put itself above the Law was the people's ignorance. At the time, very few people could read. So the church would tell the people what the holy books said and what that meant. Thus they became the authority of the Word of God. We see the exact same thing today. Though most of us can read, the word of Law has been made so complex, convoluted, and written with so much jargon that the ordinary individual is incapable of reading and understanding it, even if they had the time to do so. So we, as a society, have gone back to relying on "the experts" to interpret and navigate the Law for us. Just like we used to rely on the church, the priests, rabbis, and other holy men to give us the Word of God, now we seek out the lawyers to tell us what the law says. Subsequently, here we are, again, at the mercy of a small group of individuals whose intentions are…well…their own…whatever those are.

In a modern society, the Law should be

1. easy to understand, so anyone with the basic ability to read can understand it for themselves;
2. administered by the common people, so no small group is relied upon for its enforcement or interpretation; and

3. applicable to everyone, regardless of position or status. (Even God should be subject to the Law—well definitely his followers, at least.)

So how do we do this? First of all, we simplify the Law. We create a set of Laws that are simply written and easy to understand. Not unlike the Ten Commandments. This is the initial list I've come up with. It is against the Law to

- kill a person;
- injure a person or society;
- bear false witness, commit perjury, or knowingly disseminate disinformation;
- compel a person against their will without consent;
- take or give that which does not legally belong to you;
- commit treason against society;
- discriminate based upon any criteria that a person has no control over (i.e., race, sex, cultural background, etc.), or by which every person's perspective is unique (i.e., relationship with God, sexual preference, self-image, etc.);
- deprive a person of their ability to worship; and
- use the Law as a weapon or for personal or private gains. Civil matters are to be heard in the civil arena.

This is most likely not a comprehensive list. But these few can deal with the majority of issues people face today. The broad brushstroke nature of the Law allows for most situations. Ideas for implementing this will be outlined later.

Ethics

Ethics have been a heated point of discussion for many centuries and go hand in hand with the Law. The *Oxford English Dictionary* basically defines ethics as "moral principles that govern a person's behavior of an activity."

Usually, the discussion of ethics involves some sticky ethical question about whether a certain choice is "ethical" or not. The problem with this approach is that there is no baseline to operate from. Everyone's perception is a little different, and so everyone feels differently about it. Thus the discussions rage on, and no answer is ever really obtained. Sure there are many things that have just been designated as unethical, and those extreme cases have been largely established. It's the smaller questions—questions of everyday behavior—or questions of life or death that give us trouble. So to establish an ethical baseline for society to operate from, I propose the following:

- To burden or allow someone to be burdened without consent is unethical.
- Your actions imply consent to all the repercussions of that action.

When ethical questions are examined from this baseline, much of the discussion goes away. Now, not being a professor of ethics, I'm sure there are situations that may befuddle this baseline. Nothing is perfect. Every rule has its exceptions. But operating from a simple baseline is important, as this provides a solid foundation for behavior that everyone can understand.

Implementation of the Law

The second element of separating Law and State is to turn the implementation and interpretation of the Law over to the common people. Once the Law has been simplified and an ethical baseline has been established, this can be done through the use of the jury and citizen judges. Since the Law is accessible to everyone and a societal ethical baseline has been established, every citizen can be tasked with its implementation. Each case will be tried individually and without consideration of precedent. Lawyers will debate and mediate the pros and cons of the case between the parties to determine the severity of the violation. It is here where former successful arguments (precedent) might be made use of, though the former decision will not be taken into consideration in the actual case. A jury selected anonymously and at random from the citizenry in the local area where the Law was violated will decide guilt or innocence. Then a citizen judge, also selected randomly from the local citizenry, will determine the sentence and/or punishment. Judges will also be held accountable to the Law and ethical baseline for their judgments. Other citizen judges will rejudge each sentence to ensure that the sentences are appropriate.

This is a very broad brushstroke view of how a new legal system might work. Details about logistics and nuances will be detailed later.

The important aspect of this system is that it removes the need for "the expert." This will make it much more difficult for an individual or group to put themselves in a position to manipulate the system and put themselves above the Law. Thus it limits the consolidation of power in any group or individual.

Make no mistake. I have great faith in humanity's ability to figure out a method to manipulate any system and attempt to put themselves above others. It is, after all, what we do. But this system empowers everyone to hold those people accountable.

The Legal System

Since the ultimate foundation of any society is the Law, let's begin with that. As described above, the Law should be simply put and understandable by anyone with the basic ability to read. To maintain freedom, the Law must be exclusive, not inclusive (i.e., the Law must describe only that which is illegal as opposed to what is legal). The list of basic Laws described above is by no means complete, though it should cover the majority of situations, and, as always, exceptions to every rule will certainly exist. But taken along with an ethical baseline, as exampled above, I believe societies can create and implement a system of Law that suits any culture. But I'll leave it to those implementing this system in their society to be the final arbiters of their Law.

There's no reason to reinvent the wheel. Much of what came before works just fine. Enforcement and prosecution of the Law will follow much of the same system we already have in place. Our current system of jurisprudence actually works pretty well, with the exception of a few glaring problems. Almost all of them stem from the problem we've already discussed. The lack of accountability for malfeasance or wrongdoing within the system itself. The cause of this problem stems primarily from the current Law being too complex (thus the need for experts), and too much power is being bestowed on a few people for too long a time. It's a well-known concept that power corrupts, and the longer power is held, the more likely corruption will occur. So how do we accommodate this very human failing? We grant this power for a very limited time and in a random fashion. People in positions prone to corruption are not empowered long enough to do much damage or position themselves in a place of unassailable power. Since the places are filled randomly and cases are heard randomly, the ability to corrupt or persuade any particular case becomes far more difficult. The system works like this.

1. There is an accusation of the Law being broken. This can come from anyone and can be levied against anyone.

2. Law enforcement takes a statement from the accuser and any other relevant witnesses or involved parties. Law enforcement then decides whether further legal action is warranted and acts accordingly (i.e., make an arrest, issue a citation, issue a warning, initiate an investigation, mediate the dispute, etc.).

3. Should Law enforcement deem further legal action necessary, the accused will be arrested, detained, or ordered to appear. Should an accused party be arrested, they will be allowed to appear before a judge and plead for bail, supervised release, an order to appear, etc., with the benefit of council if desired.

4. The accuser will then be provided a short period of time to prepare their accusation with the benefit of council, if desired. Pro bono council will be provided, at society's expense, to anyone wishing for it but unable to acquire private council. Then both sides are given the opportunity and encouraged to negotiate their positions with each other and come to their own solution.

5. Should a private solution not occur, the accuser will then, under oath, present their case in written and/or recorded form to the accused party, who will respond in written and/ or recorded form. The accuser will then get a final opportunity to respond in written and/or recorded form, and the accused will get a final opportunity to respond to their response. This will constitute the case.

6. The case will then be presented to an appropriate court, judge, and jury, who will review the written and/or recorded testimony and statements. Based on the case, the jury will decide guilt or innocence. In the case of a guilty verdict, the jury will determine a level of severity that will be attached for the judge's consideration. A guilty verdict must have no less than a 3/4 quorum of the jurors. Capital cases involving life or death require unanimous verdicts. Less than a 3/4 guilty verdict is an acquittal, with the ability to appeal granted to the accuser. Each case is allowed one and only one appeal.
7. If a guilty verdict is rendered, the judge will then render a sentence that will be governed by a suggested set of sentencing guidelines.
8. Should a not guilty verdict be rendered, the accuser will be held responsible for all costs and damages incurred by the accused during this process.

All cases will be heard as individual instances without consideration of precedent or similar past cases. The burden of proof lies with the accuser. The accused is to be considered and treated as innocent until judged guilty by a jury. All guilty cases are to be reviewed by the next higher court, with the district court being the highest and last word.

Guilty cases are allowed one appeal to the next higher-level court. Appeals will be reviewed by a jury and deemed valid or overturned. If deemed valid, the original ruling and sentence will stand. The jury may decide to overturn the verdict or decide that the sentence was inappropriate. In which case, a new judge will resentence the case.

Cases may be reheard at the same level as the original case should new evidence arise, which could change the outcome. A case being reheard will start over at the beginning of the process, with the accuser or accused resubmitting their case for negotiation with the addition of the new evidence. The process will progress forward from there.

A case being reheard will be heard by a new jury and judge. If a case is reheard and overturned and a guilty party is found innocent, the accusing party will be held responsible for costs and damages incurred by the accused, including all the time since the original verdict.

There are no statutes of limitations on violations of the Law.

The Jury

All accusations have the Right to be heard by a jury. Juries are selected at random and anonymously via lottery from the citizenry of the geographic area between the ages of eighteen and seventy where the accusation occurred and depending on the court hearing the case (see "Courts and Judges"). Juries will consist of twelve citizens and will serve for a term of ten business days or two cases, whichever comes first.[8] A random and anonymously selected pool of jurors will be called, and then specific juries will be randomly and anonymously selected from that pool as needed. Called jurors will be notified that they have been called into the pool of potential jurors, but they will only need to report if they are selected to hear a case.

Jury duty is one of the foundational pillars of a civilized society. Employers will be required to provide fully paid leave for selected jurors. Once a juror has been called into the juror pool and fulfilled either the ten days or two cases, their name will be removed from the juror/judge lottery for two years.

---

[8] Judges and juries actively involved in a case may be required to serve past the ten business days in order to properly adjudicate the case.

A Question of Jury Impartiality

The question of a completely impartial jury has been promoted as one of the important aspects of our current jury system. Though it is good in principle, our complexity as humans, with our myriad of prejudices, moral beliefs, societal pressures, and the like, makes being perfectly impartial on any matter a near impossibility for any of us. We all have an opinion about pretty much everything. So though the concept of impartiality is good, the reality is otherwise. Currently, in practice, the process of jury selection is not about finding an impartial jury but getting as sympathetic a jury to your cause or case as possible. Therefore, the quest to find an impartial jury should be abandoned, and juries should be selected completely at random from the communities affected. What this will do is enforce the local values of the affected communities, so crimes may be punished or enforced with varying degrees of severity depending on the values of the community in which they were committed. This should inhibit the values of powers outside the community from overly prejudicing how a community wishes to handle its own internal issues. It is important, though, that the impulsion to enforce the law outside the court (i.e., vigilantism) be discouraged, for the results of that have been shown to be very detrimental.[9]

Therefore, it is theorized here, based on a basic understanding of social psychology, that if justice is meted out by a community, operating largely under the values of that community and governed by widely understood laws and an ethical baseline, members of the community will have a higher level of trust in the court to dispense justice according to communal standards and values and be less apt to seek justice outside the system. This should create a higher level of trust and compliance within the community toward law enforcement and the courts. However, it is also important to limit the ability of a community to promote vastly prejudiced policies within itself. This can be largely accomplished by holding judges accountable to the Law for judgments, reviewing judgments by higher courts, and specifying sentencing guidelines for judges. Therefore, communities may have varying punishments for similar crimes based on specific community values, but no community will have the right to excessively punish any particular crime.

---

[9]   Greenshields, (1994), 231.

Courts and Judges

Courts will be established by population. One local court for every ≈ 2,500 people located in an area (these numbers may need to be adjusted to facilitate case load), one regional court for every ≈ 10,000 people within a regional area, one sectional court for ≈ 100,000 people, and one district court for every 1,000,000 people. A special tribunal court may be called in cases involving crimes against society as a whole (i.e., treason, government misappropriation of authority or power, terrorism against society, crimes affecting societal infrastructure like large-scale banking fraud or malfeasance, mass dissemination of misinformation, etc.).

Judges will be selected at random and anonymously via lottery from the citizenry between the ages of forty-five and seventy years of age from the geographic area where they reside for each court. Judges will serve for a period of ten business days or two cases, whichever comes first.[10] Judges may serve only one court at a time. Once a judge has been called and fulfilled their obligation, they will be removed from the juror/judge lottery for a period of two years. Judges will be compensated for their time as judges at a daily rate that is appropriate considering current daily compensation rates, and employers will be required to provide fully paid leave for selected judges.

---

[10] Judges and juries actively involved in a case may be required to serve past the ten business days in order to properly adjudicate the case.

Court Purview

Each court will be responsible for hearing cases concerning its populace's area. Small localized crimes, such as petty theft, an isolated attack, domestic issues, etc., will be heard by the local courts. Crimes involving a larger section of the community will be heard by the regional or sectional courts, depending on the extent of the crime (fraud, grand theft, serial crimes, crimes involving numerous victims, etc.).

The regional and sectional courts will also hear appeals from the courts directly below them. Appeals at the district level will be heard by another district court. All cases are allowed one appeal, unless new evidence is being presented. In which case, a new case and hearing process will be initiated.

Citizenship

I've referred to "citizens" in the previous section about the Law, and everyone has an idea of what a citizen is. In this country, a citizen is anyone born here. Oh, of course, it's possible to achieve citizenship through a process if one immigrates, but these are not the citizens I'm going to refer to in this section. In this society, citizenship is largely taken for granted. Well, that's because it is…granted. Very few give any thought to what being a citizen is or means, or what responsibilities or obligations go along with that. It's just something given to you at birth, and no one can take it away from you. Typically, all anyone thinks about is, *What am I entitled to*? And most feel that they're entitled to much more than they actually are.

Automatic or "free" citizenship is a problem. As with anything that is given away freely to all, it loses its value. Most natural-born citizens give very little thought to what it means to be a citizen. Currently, in most public schools, things like civics, citizenship, and the Constitution aren't even taught. It seems to me most citizens believe being a citizen means "I do what I want!"

In a healthy society, the members of that society—the citizens— understand what it means to be a citizen. Holding that position is important and requires a certain level of behavior and commitment to yourself and society as a whole.

According to the US Citizenship and Immigration website, the following are the responsibilities of a US citizen:

- Support and defend the Constitution.
- Stay informed about the issues affecting your community.
- Participate in the democratic process.
- Respect and obey federal, state, and local laws.
- Respect the Rights, opinions, and beliefs of others.
- Participate in your local community.
- Pay income and other taxes honestly and on time to federal, state, and local authorities.
- Serve on a jury when called.
- Defend the country if the need arises.

If you're reading this, chances are you're a conscientious individual who takes their position in society seriously, and you are looking to make positive changes to our society. But let's take a really hard look at these nine things from a societal perspective and judge ourselves on what level of citizenry we really have.

Support and defend the Constitution. Okay, that seems like a pretty easy one. But how many have *actually* read the Constitution? Sure many say they read it in school, but not anymore. Most schools don't teach the Constitution. If you read it in school, let's say as a freshman in high school, how many years ago was that? And how much did you actually retain and incorporate? Do you know the differences between the Declaration of Independence, the Preamble, the Constitution, and the Bill of Rights? What does each present or grant? I imagine that even among this audience, those are challenging questions. Imagine how those questions will fall on ordinary citizens. I just imagine a lot of blank stares.

Stay informed about the issues affecting your community. Actually, I think most people do their best with this one, especially in today's society of immediate media. It's pretty easy to find out what's going on, and I think most folks try to stay abreast of what's going on. However, how accurate or important is that information? The computer, the source of much of our information these days, tracks what we look for. Then based on our search histories and viewing patterns, the algorithm presents us with more information similar to what we historically looked at. This then creates a situation where we're mostly given more of what we want to hear as opposed to receiving balanced and opposing views on issues. Without opposing views, our opinions appear to continually be validated, which then cements that particular opinion in our heads as fact, whether it's actually true or not. As we become more and more convinced that what we believe is correct because the computer keeps giving us validating information, we become less and less willing to consider the validity of opposing thoughts, opinions, and ideas. An unwillingness to consider opposing positions only creates dissension among the people because everyone is convinced that they are "right." Why wouldn't they believe they're right? The computer has validated their positions over and over, regardless of the position. The ideological divide this country and its communities are currently seeing is in no small part a result of everyone being convinced that they're "right."

No one likes to admit when they're wrong. But being wrong, or admitting you don't know, is the only path to learning. We should be proud if we don't know something, and we should welcome someone who has a reason to make us question what we think we know. Otherwise, we'll just continue to wallow in our own righteous ignorance and never grow beyond what we are today. It's interesting that trying to stay informed of the issues in our community may have become the root of many of the issues in our community. It's worth a thought before we move on.

Participate in the democratic process. This one nearly makes me laugh. This is as simple as getting out and voting. With the exception of our last presidential election (Biden vs. Trump in 2020), voter turnout is abysmal, with it being below 30 percent in many cases. How can anyone believe that our elected representatives are representative when nearly 3/4 of the "citizenry" isn't even participating? I'm sure there's an entire volume about why people aren't participating in the process, but I think it comes down to one primary thing—people don't feel their vote counts—so why bother? Another issue, I believe, stems from the quality of our elected officials. Why vote when the choices we're given are so discouraging? But not participating is violating your responsibility as a citizen. But hey, who cares? What are they going to do? Take my citizenship away if I don't vote? Well, maybe we should.

Respect and obey federal, state, and local laws. I'm not going to spend any time on this, as we've already discussed the Law and how and why it's obeyed.

Respect the Rights, beliefs, and opinions of others. Though this may sound pretty simple, this is actually a really tough one. Respecting the position of someone whose ideas are completely opposite of yours is a really tough ask. We all feel very strongly about our personal beliefs. Granting someone the space to completely disagree with you can be challenging, to say the least. At one time, differing opinions were often seen as opportunities for debate, discussion, and growth. But it seems that in recent times, dogma and intolerance have become the order of the day. When intelligent, well-educated people are destroying friendships of decades over political biases, this is not respect for another's beliefs. When authorities violate an individual's Rights because of their skin color or social demographic, this is not respect for one's Rights. Of all the responsibilities and duties of citizenship, this may be the most difficult because it requires you to allow for the possibility that your position, opinion, or belief may be wrong. However, at the same time, it may be the most important, as the only time anything new can be learned is when you admit that you really don't know or that what you think you know or believe may be wrong. It is the responsibility and duty of citizens to accept this. Unfortunately, it seems most of today's "citizens" are a long way from it.

Participate in your local community. This one is a no-brainer. If you're living your life, doing your business, and doing what you do, you're participating in your community. That's what community is—people doing their things, and somehow it all gets mashed together to make up communities of all sorts. If you want to see a perfect example, just stand on a street corner in Manhattan. Millions of folks are all going about their business, and how it all mashes together creates the community. Some may argue that it is more specific than that and that it means doing altruistic or charitable things in your community. Those are great things and definitely give a community a friendlier, more open feel, and I encourage everyone to participate in those activities, but that's not what it's really all about. It's about you making your specific value available to the rest of us. So on this point, I believe we're doing pretty well.

Pay income and other taxes honestly and on time to federal, state, and local authorities. If we're just looking at how well our citizens are upholding their responsibilities, I wonder how we'd do without the three most terrifying letters in the English language—IRS. Most citizens pay their taxes, but I contend that most only do it out of fear of the IRS. I wonder how many would actually do it if the IRS didn't exist. Okay, I'll stop saying IRS. Studies have shown that even mentioning the IRS can make people nervous and uneasy. Think about that the next time you're paying taxes. Are you paying taxes to support and grow your society, or are you doing it out of fear of reprisals from an entity that has been essentially above any accountability?

Serve on a jury when called. Personally, I consider this one of the most important responsibilities of the citizenry. The jury is the most direct way an individual, or group of individuals, can reign in injustices and participate in creating an equitable and just society. However, most consider it to be an inconvenient burden and will, literally, do almost anything to get out of doing it. Why is this?

I believe having your transgressions evaluated by the members of society affected by your actions is a good way to measure the severity of your transgressions. As a citizen, it seems that it should be viewed as almost a sacred honor to participate in this very important role. But alas, it seems that most people do not view it that way.

Defend the country if the need should arise. Of all these, I believe this one is the one that we're actually most prepared and willing to do. I believe that almost everyone will step up to defend the nation if the need actually arises. Hell, many of us are actively preparing for it. So I'm not going to spend any time on this.

So now that we've taken a look at the essential duties and responsibilities of a citizen, I've made the proposition that most people don't take their duties as citizens very seriously, if at all. So we have to ask ourselves why. Why are our responsibilities as citizens viewed with such indifference or, in some cases, outright animosity? The answer seems simple to me. First, we didn't have to do anything to get it. It was just given to us at birth for nothing more than being lucky enough to have been born here. Second, we don't have to do anything to keep it. We can break every rule of society, deny, and ignore every duty and responsibility of a citizen, and even go so far as to commit treason against our society, and we'll still maintain our citizenship. And third, it can't be taken away from us. If there's ever been a situation where something could be "taken for granted," well, this is it. Why? Because it *is* granted. And since it's granted, who cares? What difference does it make?

It is this author's opinion that this is the reason why the citizenry of this country is so unconcerned about being a citizen. Oh, we'll demand our Rights and privileges of citizenship, often in violent fashion, if we perceive they're being violated, but ask someone to be on a jury or…vote. Oh, that's too much of an inconvenience or bother. The value of being a citizen has been degraded all the way to less than worthless, even though it may be one of the most valuable things we as Americans have. Ask any immigrant who has fled a life without Rights or freedom and worked to obtain citizenship. If you ask me, these people are the most truly American people today. They understand the value of citizenship and are honored to participate. The vast majority of "natural-born" citizens simply don't value what they have simply because it didn't cost them anything to get it. They've never been without it, and it can never be taken away. This is why citizen participation is so abysmal.

So what is the solution? Citizenship must be earned. Details of this will be discussed in the next section.

Citizenship II

Since fundamental human, legal, and civil Rights apply to all persons and should be protected and enforced by the Law, citizenship becomes a choice of the acceptance of certain duties and responsibilities fundamental to the functioning of society in exchange for additional benefits. Citizenship should be granted to any person above the age of eighteen who chooses to complete a two-year citizenship training program. The completion of the citizenship training program will entitle and obligate the new citizen to the following benefits and responsibilities (this may not be a comprehensive list):

Citizen Responsibilities:

- Participation in the democratic process, which means voting in every voting session.
- Participation in the national defense if needed. This only applies to attacks on our sovereign soil, not foreign military actions.
- Faithfully performing judge or jury duties.
- Receiving 160 hours of continuing education every two years until the age of fifty.

Citizen Benefits:

- Two years of post–high school education
- Gun ownership
- Militia membership, if desired
- Public officer eligibility
- Law enforcement officer eligibility
- Military officer eligibility
- Deportation and embassy protection internationally
- Extended international travel privileges
- Enhanced social security benefits

Citizenship Disqualifications:

- Conviction of any felony.
- Failure to fulfill the duties of a citizen when called upon.
- Citizenship may be reinstated after any sentence has been completed and recompletion of the citizenship training program has been completed.

Citizenship Training Program

The citizenship training program is a two-year full-time service and education program. Participants will be provided room and board, along with compensation commensurate with that of enlisted soldiers of similar service periods. Participants must pass basic aptitude qualifications, including basic reading, writing, speaking in English (or society's native language), and mathematics to the basic algebra level. Applicants failing to pass the aptitude qualifications will be provided education in areas needing improvement until the basic qualifications can be met.

Any person above the age of eighteen is eligible.

The training program will consist of an education section including civics, the Law, legal processes and procedures, government structure and procedures, the Constitution (as developed for the new society, not the 1787 one.), and general history (here is where the 1787 Constitution could be studied). The training program will also include two thousand hours of service. This service can be social (assisting with social programs for people needing assistance), community (maintaining public areas), political (acting as pages and aides to government officials), industrial (apprenticing for a civilian-owned business), or military (military training will include the citizen education program and honorable military service; beyond two years, will grant citizenship).

Citizen's Role in Government

The fundamental premise of a democratic republic is to be a representative voice of the People to the government during the decision-making process of governing. This is typically done by using the vote. There are many ways the People can vote. A ballot containing a certain number of choices for a specific question or questions can be used. How and where the People choose to spend their money is a type of vote. People's actions, either in compliance or in disobedience, are also a type of vote. The right to strike, assemble, and protest, either peacefully or otherwise, are also forms of voting. Any way the People can make their voices and concerns heard by the people making decisions is a form of voting.

As described earlier, one of the fundamental responsibilities of a Citizen is to participate in the democratic process. In a modern society, the voices and concerns of the governed must be considered in all decision-making processes, both in government and industry.

Industry is easy. The market, or vote by dollar, is the only and final arbiter of all industry decisions. Industry must, of course, be regulated in their methods of obtaining that vote (i.e., how they get the money). Oftentimes, if left to their own devices, industry can exploit or manipulate the available resources for short-term gains at the expense of the long-term well-being of society and the market.

The government is a little more difficult. Where industry's objective is to make money effectively, government's objective is to spend money effectively. How and where to spend that money can be a very tricky question.

Enter the politician.

The *Oxford English Dictionary* defines "politician" as "a person who is professionally involved in politics, especially as a holder of or a candidate for an elected office."

Oxford defines "politics" as "the activities associated with the governance of a country or other area, specifically the debate or conflict among individuals or parties having or hoping to achieve power."

Essentially, and as simply put as possible, politicians decide how the government is going to spend its money. The amount of money any one politician can direct translates directly into political power. Politicians spend their professional work days debating, discussing, and deciding where the government's money is going to be spent. Each politician vies for funding for their areas of interest, be that their represented districts or constituencies or other personal or professional projects. Their success in these debates typically translates directly to greater political power and influence.

All democratic systems to date utilize some sort of voting process to select an individual to fill the role of a politician and represent the voter's interests in the political debates about the spending of the government's money (tax money). Unfortunately, we run right back into the fundamental problem with all human systems—humans.

A Good Idea That
Just Didn't Work

Consider the word "politician." When asked, most people consider the word politician to have a negative connotation. Ask what they think when they hear the word "politician," and most people will answer "dishonest," "untrustworthy," "liar," "self-interested," "greedy," "power hungry," etc. A word in a language doesn't achieve a seemingly universal connotation overnight. This suggests that politicians, or at least the people who have been in the position of politicians, have been of questionable quality for a very long time. Even Shakespeare wrote: "Get thee glass eyes, and like a scurvy politician, seem to see the things thou dost not" (King Lear, Act 4, Sc. 6).

I attribute this, at least in this country, to something our founding fathers just didn't expect when they were setting up their new democratic republic. A democratic republic is a particular form of representative government where specific groups of people are represented by one or a few individuals. In our case, that individual(s) is selected by vote of the represented peoples and then sent to the capital to speak for them on matters of governance. On its face, this seems very reasonable. The founding fathers assumed that, given the opportunity, people would select their best to represent them. Unfortunately, this didn't turn out to be the case. It seems what has happened is that instead of communities selecting a representative who truly represents their values and beliefs, individuals with their own agendas actively seek to convince the voters to vote for them regardless of their own agendas or the needs of the community.

Oftentimes, these individuals will use any means necessary, including lying, bad-mouthing, and other marketing techniques, to "get the vote." And the techniques get dirtier and more severe the higher the office trying to be achieved. Rumors of murder, blackmail, and extortion have been reported as techniques for achieving some of the highest offices. Though hard evidence of these techniques is rare, the old saying "politics is a dirty business" is not without merit. What has resulted is that all too often, candidates with charisma and marketing skills who are competent at getting elected are being put into positions of power, but they may not be competent to actually represent, govern, or lead effectively. Having the skills required to get elected doesn't necessarily mean you have the skills to govern. All too often, modern elections seem to be nothing more than popularity contests and about those who can stir up political fervor, instead of platforms, problems, qualifications, solutions, or leadership. One study showed that people consistently voted for the more physically attractive candidate. This system naturally and often attracts individuals with designs on obtaining power for themselves who may or may not be overly concerned about representative responsibilities.

As I listen to the various pundits, newscasters, podcasters, and political analysts, I keep hearing the same theme. All of them, regardless of which side they speak for, are constantly discussing the actions and failings of these elected officials. It has become obvious to me that relying on the People to select someone to make decisions for the whole, based on nothing more than a simple popularity contest and marketing campaign, is a poor way to select a qualified individual to fill any role. A modern society should be governed by individuals qualified to lead and govern—individuals who rise to positions of leadership through achievement, skill, and competency, not by winning a popularity contest. The best leaders may not always be the most popular people.

Since political power is one of the most powerful types of power, the quest for it naturally attracts those hungry for power, and those hungry for power seem to be the most susceptible to the corrupt-ing influences of power. So all too often, candidates seeking political power, once elected and achieving some level of power, begin to be corrupted by the power. The longer they stay in power, the more corrupt they usually become. So what we eventually, all too often, end up with is a charismatic person able to convince voters, usually too busy with their own lives to pay much attention, wielding con-siderable power over long periods of time, and often succumbing to whatever temptations that power may offer. It generates a self-pro-moting cycle. As an individual's time and power in office increase, their influence over other politicians increases, which then increases their ability to influence the decisions of lesser politicians, and on and on until it's possible to get into an unassailable position of power and influence where only the most egregious abuses are questioned.

So a modern society, understanding what allure and potential political power represent, should implement a system that promotes competence in the administration of government and hinders those seeking to obtain political power for their own purposes while ensur-ing that the People's voice is still heard.

Obsolescence of the Ruler

Throughout nature, all communal creatures live in a sort of despotic autocracy. Beehives and ant colonies live to serve their queen. Mammalian animal societies are lorded over by "the alpha," the strongest and often most aggressive male in the pack. These are the basic survival tactics. In the insect world, the queen is a unique individual, physically, with the ability to lay eggs and thus replenish the hive or colony population. In mammalian packs, the strongest male is the one who typically breeds with the females, ensuring that the strongest genes are passed on and thus strengthening the pack as a whole.

Humans, being mammals, have followed, more or less, this pattern for millennia. Almost without exception, nearly every human society has been arranged with an "alpha" of sorts in the form of king, emperor, president, general, etc. These alphas were almost always male and often imbued with the power or authority of God. In some societies, these alphas were even granted the Right of *prima nocta*, which means the king, or pretty much any noble, had the Right to have sex with any of their female subjects, regardless of their will or marital status. Fortunately, for all women and their partners, this practice was eventually abandoned. Though it is impossible to say for sure, it's very likely the practice in itself led to such subject discontent that it may have been a major factor in uprisings and overthrows of many rulers—a sort of self-defeating policy. Regardless, humans, for many centuries, have organized themselves according to this natural pattern.

As human society has grown and developed, the direct influence of the "alpha" on the lives of the individual members of society has grown less and less. Our leaders, rulers, presidents, etc. now concern themselves largely with the concerns of the state and less with the individual members of society. If you take a moment to consider the quality of your life throughout your life, then ask yourself, *Did my life change in any significant manner as a result of the changing of the presidents or congress?* If you live in the United States, most likely the answer will be "no." That may be due to our stable form of government, which has allowed a smoothness of life…for lack of a better description.

But even in a place like Russia, which has gone through massive government and leadership changes in the last one hundred years, life at the bottom, so to speak, goes on largely unchanged. They've gone from an ancient autocracy to militaristic communist rule, to a democratically elected president, to warring warlords and gangsters, and now to a militaristic dictatorship, with numerous revolts and revolutions between each. Meanwhile, the lives of the ordinary people on the street really haven't changed all that much. Things were hard and scarce. They continued to be hard and scarce, and they are currently relatively hard and scarce. Russia is, largely, a hard and difficult place to live. Its people are likewise tough and adapted to life there. Despite the individual(s) who happen to occupy the Kremlin at any time, the people live their lives as they have for hundreds of years and, I believe, will continue to do so long into the future.

The point is that as human society has developed and we further and further separate ourselves from the law of nature, the need for an alpha has become increasingly obsolete. Human society, being as complex as it is, definitely needs to be managed. It just doesn't need to be ruled. I would make the argument that attempting to rule it is complete folly at this point.

The point should be made here that this theory of ruler obsolescence only applies to societies that have achieved a certain level of civilization. This will not work in places where society is still at a primitive or barbaric stage. Places where violence over petty squabbles, boundaries or ideologies interfere with the healthy development and growth of society as a whole. In these environments, individuals are still consumed with basic survival or their own short-term self-interest at the expense of all else. In these cases, an alpha with a larger vision is required to bring about the understanding that working together will get us all higher than trying to climb over each other ever will. This author considers these types of societies primitive societies, and these theories will not work for them.

Now, that being said, on any scale smaller than a societal scale, the need for leaders and leadership is undeniable. Therefore, the management of society should fall to smaller autonomous departments, each dedicated to specific elements of societal management. In this way, the various necessities of society can be managed by people with expertise in those specific necessities. These departments can then be organized using currently well-established management and hierarchy principles used in organizations and businesses that have proven to work well for decades. As societal issues begin to approach the national level, such as issues of national security, defense, trade, international relations, etc. These issues can be dealt with by a group of leaders from each department concerned.

In this manner, a society can do away with the individual ruler, who, at their will, may drive the society into an unhealthy place. Many of the founding fathers argued vehemently against the creation of an individual president on the basis that the office could be imbued with too much power and could become kinglike. In his book *Fear and Loathing on the Campaign Trail '71*, political correspondent Hunter S. Thompson wrote:

> A career politician finally smelling the White
> House is not much different from a bull elk in
> rut. He will stop at nothing, trashing anything
> that gets in his way; and anything he can't handle
> personally, he will hire out, or failing that make
> a deal. It is a difficult syndrome for most people

to understand, because so few of us ever come close to the kind of ultimate power and achievement that the White House represents to a career politician.

This is just one perspective on the potential dangers of a single ruler. In recent years, many societies around the world, the United States included, have experienced firsthand the chaos and unrest that not only a divisive or overly ambitious leader or president can create, but even the chaos and sometimes violence that the selection or election process of such an individual can manifest.

It may be better to just do away with it all together and divest that power to a larger group of people with specific expertise and the ability to check the power of any individual or small group.

Eliminating the Elected Official

For reasons discussed earlier, it seems that much of the trouble with government is "rule by the elected official."

The people who work in government—those who weren't elected but hired—usually seem to be competent in their specific area of expertise. Managers, functionaries, clerks, and bureaucrats usually have a pretty good idea of how to get things done within their specific departments. Many problems seem to arise when a newly elected official shows up without any experience or training and begins to try to manage and run a department without much or any understanding of how things are already being done. Or someone is promoted beyond their capacity through either political wrangling, nepotism, or the Peter Principle.[11] Another common issue is that incumbents who may have an understanding of how a system is operating stop managing because they're focusing on keeping their job (getting reelected) as opposed to actually doing the job they were elected to do.

Essentially, what our representatives are supposed to be doing is directing the flow of money (tax money) back into society for the

---

[11] Laurence J. Peter, *The Peter Principle* (1969).

support and betterment of society, so a voting system that directs the money flow instead of electing people to direct it could be utilized.

How this would work is that each citizen receives a ballot periodically (twice a year or so). The ballot will have all the sections of the government on it (see "The Government" section). The voter will then number the sections one to whatever (depending on how many governmental sections there end up being), with one being the most important to the voter and on down to the least important to the voter. These ballots will then be collected and the numbers tabulated. Then based on those numbers, the budget is allocated between the various sections of the government. This system could be used at all levels of government. The ballots could be tabulated at the local level, sent to the county, then to the state, then to the federal. Using a single ballot like this will also facilitate auditing the voting process, as ballot numbers will be recorded in many stages along the way.

Politicians and lobbyists can then go to work within the government sections to vie for funding within each individual section. Funding from one section will not be able to be diverted to another section. Each section must operate within the funding the People have decided to give it. This is not a huge diversion from the current system. It simply eliminates the power given to any one individual by being elected to office.

The list of other things this system will eliminate is as long as my arm. Some of the more notable things to be eliminated will be political campaigns and speeches, campaign contributions, elections…and all that goes along with those, pork fat bills, political parties (or at least the two-party system we have now), voter fraud (or the accusation of it), and on and on. All these problems stem from the competitive win or lose, one side or the other aspect of our current election process. Without that two-sided win-or-lose aspect, all these problems disappear.

Putting the direction of the money directly into the hands of the governed will further dilute the ability for individuals to consolidate power and money into one place, thus reducing the chance that someone will be able to obtain great or unassailable amounts of power.

Through this system, politicians and lobbyists will still have important work to do, but they won't be in a position of power or control and probably won't be elected at all. The people actually making the decisions will be people working in the actual departments with boots-on-the-ground experience whose jobs don't rely on getting reelected but on how well they are able to handle their budgets and projects. This change to a government meritocracy will be discussed in the next section.

I believe a system like this will eliminate much of the power currently associated with the position of politician. Eventually, the position will begin to attract people interested in the progress of society or communities, not so much those seeking a path to power.

Once again, let's take the word "politician." Imagine that it didn't have the negative connotation as discussed above, but it had the same connotation as the word "veteran." Since both politicians and veterans are essentially tasked with similar responsibilities, namely, the care and well-being of the country or society as a whole, I see no reason why they shouldn't share the same level of respect. All we need to do is change how politicians are placed and controlled. Veterans enjoy a certain level of respect, largely in my opinion, because they served. No one joins the military as a track to power, and few achieve any level of power while serving in the military. Many join politics as a track to power, and one can achieve some level of power very quickly if handled properly. If politics wasn't such a path to power and was a role focused on serving the People and society, I believe society would view politicians in a much more positive light. Just imagine Politicians' Day.

A Warning

Fear of the unknown is a basic emotion all humans experience, to some extent or another. It is one of our basic survival instincts. Humans have developed numerous methods for dealing with this potentially crippling emotion. Unfortunately some of the methods can quickly undermine positive societal progress. Because these methods promise potential protection or solutions to this very basic biological human feeling, people often follow or adopt them in an attempt to alleviate or eliminate this fear.

These things are dogma, ideology, and righteousness. All three, basically, adopt a rigid set of ideals and deny any other perspective. Essentially, all three reduce the conditions of the world to a manageable set of "known or controllable" elements. All else is then deemed "evil, wrong, backward, inferior, sinful," etc. In this way, we can create an illusion consisting of a limited number of elements that are manageable by our limited intellects. All of us do this to some extent or another, as dealing with the infinite number of possibilities the world consists of is overwhelming to anyone.

The problem with staunch dogma, ideology, and righteousness is that they do not allow for adaptation or new, novel information, especially that which may be contrary to the precepts of the established doctrine. This unwillingness to consider alternate perspectives has led to some of the greatest atrocities known to man and may be responsible for holding back the development of much of human society for thousands of years. For many centuries, the dogma of Christianity deemed scientific study to be heresy. Such historical scientific notables as Galileo, Copernicus, and Einstein, among others, were all persecuted by the church at some point in their lives. The ideologies of the Nazis, Soviets, Chinese Communists, and many others have resulted in, unquestionably, the most horrific events in human history.

Modern societies must constantly be vigilant against the growth or development of dogmatic, ideological, or righteous elements in society. These things often germinate as appearing reasonable and logical, but then seemingly all of a sudden, the situation is out of hand and extreme things are happening, and equally extreme measures are then required to deal with them.

The Government

Earlier, we discussed the potential failings of a system run by elected officials and the idea of getting rid of them and creating a voting system where the People will vote to direct the flow of government spending directly. The ability of citizens to vote and have a voice in the functioning and operation of the government is vital in any society hoping to avoid the creation of a despotic group taking control and returning us to some form of autocratic control. Not that voting is a guarantee against such things; after all, we are humans, and there are many who will seek to place themselves or their tribe in a position of power. The Nazi party was voted into power, for example. But the vote is a hindrance to such individual ambitions. So the Right of citizens to vote must be preserved.

To effectively implement the voting system previously discussed, some basic changes in the structure of the government need to be made.

Currently, the government consists of three branches: the executive branch (essentially the decision-makers), the judiciary (the rule-makers), and the legislature (the policy-makers). Obviously, this is a very simplified description of the government, but for our purposes, it's all we need, as we're not talking about what we have but what will work better. These three branches were initially set up as autonomous arms of the government to create a system of checks and balances to keep any one branch from obtaining too much power. Unfortunately, humans have gotten a hold of it and basically turned all three branches into a single tribe, oftentimes working in conjunction with each other to consolidate power in one place. Though the powers of the different branches still retain the power to check each other, the humans within the branches, through political back-scratching, favors, appointments, threats, etc., have basically undermined the actual checks and balances originally envisioned. Party politics have essentially done away with the original checks and balances laid out by the founding fathers. Instead of voting according to their position in the government, politicians now vote along party lines, thus eliminating the separation of the three branches of government.

Earlier, we established the idea of the separation of Law and state. This would do away with the judiciary branch, leaving the executive and legislature. Since these two branches are populated largely by elected officials, what will they look like if we get rid of the elected officials?

The government should be divided into sections, much like the executive branch's cabinets. Each section will be autonomous within itself and have a specific purview of its own. These sections will probably align with the existing cabinets: departments of interior, defense, education, foreign affairs, veteran affairs, treasury, etc. Sections will be staffed by competent, qualified staff operating in a roughly military-style chain of command. Movement within the chain of command is handled by a peer review process, which will be discussed later. Currently, the top position in one of the cabinets is called secretary (i.e., secretary of defense, secretary of education, etc.). So for the purposes of this description, we'll call the top positions in our new sections the secretary, though the position can be renamed. The secretaries of each section will make up a group that will act as a ruling council and essentially perform the duties of the executive branch.

The leadership of the ruling council will shift depending on the subject matter of the current discussion. The secretary of the section whose purview concerns the current issue will act as leader of the council during those decisions, as they will be the most competent and qualified individual to make a final decision concerning any specific issue. So the leadership of the ruling council will change as various issues are discussed. This dilutes the opportunity for the consolidation of power around a single individual. Secretaries have hard-term limits of four to six years optimally, again reducing the ability to gain and consolidate power over time. After the end of their term of office, secretaries are forcibly retired from government service. This is another check against the consolidation of individual power over time.

All government employees and officers will receive the same retirement benefits as military personnel with similar amounts of time in service and rank. This eliminates the temptation of the "golden parachute" retirement currently awarded to representatives and senators.

All secretaries must be promoted from within the department in which they are leading.

Separating the government into autonomous sections or departments, as discussed above, will dilute the ability of any individual to exert pressure on anyone outside their own department. The founding fathers tried very hard to establish this, as evidenced by James Madison's February 6, 1788, letter to the *Independent Journal* that stated,

> In order to lay a due foundation for that separate and distinct exercise of the different powers of government, which to a certain extent is admitted on all hands to be essential to the preservation of liberty, it is evident that each department should have a will of its own; and consequently should be so constituted that the members of each should have as little agency as possible in the appointment of the members of the others.

Advancement through a Government Section

Since advancement in government is a path to power and can often be achieved through political, financial, familial, or other means, a system needs to be put in place to hinder the human temptation for personal advancement through means other than merit. A bureaucratic system of policy and procedure can be put in place to attempt to remove the human factor from government advancement and focus on creating a meritocracy within the government. This system begins with entrance into a government section. One should not be allowed to enter a section with a higher management level. A ranking system similar to a military ranking system will be used to create a "chain of command" within each section. Therefore, for the purpose of this discussion, we'll say that no one can enter a government section above the level of E-5 (see current military ranking systems if you're not familiar with this term).

Advancement within the section is achieved through an anonymous peer review process. At regular intervals, every employee of a section will be required to anonymously review a peer who is not directly above or below them in their chain of command but with whom they have some direct contact. For example, you will be required to review your direct supervisor's supervisor and your direct subordinate's subordinate. This way, your review doesn't affect your advancement opportunities or risk your position directly. This system is designed to reduce the ability of an individual to cajole, intimidate, bribe, politic, or advance through means other than quality work, management, and supervisory skills.

These reviews will be administered by the HR section, a section of the government in itself tasked with staffing the sections, evaluating reviews, and issuing promotion, demotion, hire, and dismiss orders, among other personnel requirements. This provides a further separation of the advancement procedure from the individual. The system should be designed so that the opportunity for promotion comes from the reviews of those above you, and the promotion itself comes from the reviews of those below you. So essentially, the door of promotion is opened by your supervisors, but you have to be lifted through the door by your subordinates. This system will facilitate the advancement of the most competent and limit the ability of people unsuited for power to advance. All positions of authority must be subject to term limits, forcing individuals up, down, or laterally. Once again, this limits the ability to consolidate power over time.

Another major change that needs to be made is the budgeting policy. Currently, government budgeting roughly works like this. A department is given its annual budget. The department then allocates that budget to its various projects for the year. At the end of the year, if they've spent all their budget, the department's budget next year is maintained or increased, regardless of whether its projects were successful or not. In essence, "use it or lose it." In many cases, it's better to not complete the project within the budgetary limitations, essentially sending the message "we need more money to do the job." This system promotes inefficiency, incompetence, waste, fraud, and theft. The $1,000 toilet seat and $2,500 hammer are results of this system. It not only promotes malfeasance with the department's money; it actually encourages and rewards it. Probably, it's not the best way to utilize the taxpayer's money.

The budgeting system must be based on performance. Departments that can allocate their budgets and effectively complete projects within the budget or under it will have their budgets maintained or increased the following year. Departments unable to effectively use their budgets will not be refunded, and "heads will roll" as the saying goes. This will promote competency, efficiency, frugality, and results in government.

These budget and project evaluations will be the purview of the HR section, again removing or granting access to money and position (both being forms of power) from individuals based on a disinterested evaluation of the project and proposed budget.

Of course, there is the possibility that the problem can spiral in the other direction. Projects given to the cheapest bidder are then subject to substandard materials, poor quality workmanship, unattainable timelines, unfinished projects, etc. Not that those don't currently exist, but replacing the tendency to overspend with the tendency to underspend certainly comes with an additional set of problems. These problems can be addressed by a systematic review of bids, the contractor's performance records, and the policy of not necessarily taking the lowest bid. These are, no doubt, difficult issues that will have to be addressed. A couple of ideas for creating checks and reviews of government spending are as follows:

- The bidding for all projects is public, and the rationale for funding decisions is included in the grant of funding.
- Projects are funded individually, as opposed to a multiple-deal package.
- All funding decisions and the individuals concerned with those decisions are matters of public record.
- All proposed projects are given a general fund account, which anyone interested in promoting the project can fund. This can reduce corruption and bribery.
- Corruption and bribery must be punished to the full extent of the law, as a violation undermining the public good.

These are just a few of the tools that may be employed to limit unauthorized spending and unfair or unsafe practices when it comes to spending government money. Of all the areas where our human tendencies are ripe for temptation, it is here with the disbursement of the massive budgets handled by the government. Much care must be taken here.

Money and Power in Government

Money and power go together like two parts of a hammer. The head is power, and the handle is money. A lot of power without any money limits the ability of power to act, and a lot of money without any power usually yields inefficient results. But put the two together in large enough quantities, and great things can happen, for good or ill. In government, both money and power are in play, and throughout history, many people have tried to gain as much as possible of both by working the political and governmental systems.

Arguably, the best form of government will be the benevolent king. A wise individual, counseled by nonambitious advisors who all have the best interests of the kingdom or society as their primary and only concern when deciding matters of state, he'd ride a unicorn, and winged pigs will fly out of his butt when he bends over. It's a nice idea, but it has no basis in reality. Usually, in the case where a small group of individuals gain control of power and money in a society, we end up with some kind of fanatic, narcissist, fascist, or dictator hell-bent on increasing their own power through slavery, intimidation, fear, or murder of everyone else. Just look at all the governments before 1700 and many today. Humans will be humans. That much power and control naturally come with many temptations, whether they be political, financial, military, sensual, or otherwise.

Not to mention the effect that kind of power often has on the human psyche. Righteousness, megalomania, and God complexes are not uncommon.

Our founding fathers were very aware of this. In the system they set up, they attempted to create a system of checks and balances to prevent any group from being able to wield too much power and money without the ability of the other branches to reign them in. Great idea. But again, humans. At the time, our founding fathers believed that the chances of one group (a political party) ever carrying a majority were remote. Of course, at the time, there were nearly a dozen political parties.

Over the past 250 years, the people elected to manage and control the money and power of the government have been able to create positions of great, even unassailable, power for themselves.

Career senators who've spent decades in office, representatives who control certain committees, presidents with individual agendas, and party leaders can exert tremendous political pressure on the rest of the representatives to vote in ways that may not be, if given the opportunity to vote their own conscience, how they would vote otherwise.

Using the anonymous peer review promotion system, as described previously, will further dilute the ability of an individual to use the promise of promotion, threat of dismissal, or demotion to politic favor or compliance.

The last problem to address is the flow of money. Here we return to the vote being designed to direct the flow of money.

Next to the jury, the People's vote is the most important aspect of any comprehensive societal governing system. The People must be allowed to have their opinions, concerns, and wishes heard by the governing body, and that governing body must be forced to consider those in its decision-making process. Our founding fathers thought that having the People send representatives to speak for them was the best way to facilitate that. Unfortunately, those individuals were all too often corrupted by the power they were given and fell into that all-too-human trap of motivated self-interest, often setting aside or at least marginalizing the wishes or best interests of the people who sent them. Playing lip service in order to "get the vote" and ensure reelection is far too common a story. Using the position to obtain, sometimes, obscene amounts of wealth is also not unusual. As it turns out, vesting a relatively small group of people with the power to decide our fates isn't working out quite as expected.

I have great faith in the ability of humans to corrupt anything they set their minds to. So I'm sure the holes in this system will be found and exploited over time. But the objective here is not to create a perfect system, just to correct and adjust some of the major flaws in the current one.

Funding the Government: A Quick History of Taxes in the US

Before 1700, essentially everything and everywhere belonged to a king. Typically, the tax collectors would come around and, in the name of the king, essentially take nearly all you had.

Our founding fathers, wanting to break that yoke, set down in their draft of the constitution that the government will be funded via taxes, duties, imposts, and excises (Art. I, Sec. 8, Clause 1). For nearly a century, the government was funded primarily through tariffs and excise taxes. Then in 1862, during the Civil War, the government needed more money to fund the war effort and levied a progressive income tax on the citizens. This tax was then abolished after the war ended. Then in 1913, Congress passed the Sixteenth Amendment, allowing for a progressive income tax to be levied on the earnings of the citizenry.

In 1935, in response to the devastating economic crash experienced in 1929 that plunged the country into a huge depression, FDR implemented the "New Deal" as an attempt to bring the country back into prosperity. The wealth tax was implemented, taking up to 75 percent of the highest incomes in taxes. Many of the wealthy took advantage of loopholes in the tax code and avoided paying these taxes. In 1937, there was a tax code reform called the Revenue Act, which tried to close some of those loopholes. In 1942, the Victory Tax was implemented to fund the WWII war effort. This was the broadest and most progressive tax in American history.

The government then began requiring employers to withhold tax directly from employees' paychecks to ease the burden of this massive tax. By the end of the war in 1945, nearly 90 percent of Americans were having taxes withheld directly from their paychecks. But, unlike the earlier 1862 version of this tax, this one was never abolished at the end of the war. This system still exists today and is a major concern for nearly all Americans living anywhere above a basic subsistence level. Today, according to the White House Office of Management and Budget, nearly 50 percent of the government's revenue comes from the individual income tax, approximately 35 percent from social insurance and retirement taxes, and the remaining 15 percent from all other sources, including corporate tax, excise, tariffs, and others. This means that over 80 percent of the government's funding comes directly out of the citizens' pockets.

What's even worse is that a 1984 report, ordered by then President Ronald Reagan and called the Grace Commission, found that 30 percent of the income tax went to pay interest on the national debt, 30 percent went uncollected, and the remainder was eaten up in waste and government inefficiency. So according to that report, none of the federal income tax goes to pay for the government services and functions we'd all expect. Not to mention the way this tax is collected. As eluded to earlier, even the mention of the IRS can cause people's heart rates and blood pressures to go up. There must be a better way.

Basic Economics

Essentially, economics is a circle. Raw materials or skills are converted into products or services that are then provided to the market in exchange for value, which then goes to pay for more raw materials or time in the case of skills and services. This is, obviously, the most basic way of looking at it. Literally, volumes, even whole schools, have been dedicated to the study and understanding of the nuances of economics, both macro and micro. But for our purposes here, we only need a very basic understanding of the circular nature of the economic process. The People's place in this circle is largely twofold. People work in industry to convert raw materials and skills into products and services and are compensated for that work. Then the people take that compensation and purchase the products and services that they need or want in their lives. Ideally, the products and services are sold for more than they cost to manufacture and/or provide, creating profit that can then be used to grow the process, and so on and so forth. Hopefully, all of you are, at this point, rolling your eyes and saying to yourself, *Well, no shit, what does this guy think we are... idiots?* If so, that's good. Because this should be obvious to everyone.

So now we come to the part that has been a matter of discussion, argument, philosophy, and often violence for many, many years. Who gets that profit, and what do they do with it? In general, there are basically two schools of thought. First, the owners of the industry or service collect the profit and use it as they see fit. This is usually referred to as capitalism or objectivism. Alternatively, the profit is taken and redistributed equitably to the workers or population in one form or another, oftentimes in the form of medical, educational, and social services, by some third party or agency, most often the government. This is usually referred to as communism or socialism. We're not going to spend any time on the third system, where one individual owns everything, takes everything, and does whatever they want. We lived with that for the entire history of civilization until 1750 or so, and I don't think anyone really wishes to go back to that.

In the last two hundred years or so, many societies have tried numerous variations of one or the other with varying degrees of success. China and the USSR attempted to build societies based on communist ideals, but both societies suffered and their "empires" crashed. China, after the Cultural Revolution, evolved into a sort of quasi-socialized capitalistic police state. By providing the world with inexpensive (essentially slave) labor and manufacturing, China was propelled into a position of world power in a relatively short period of time. Unfortunately, the quality of life for the people themselves only improved for those at the top of the pyramid, so to speak, and the rest were left to live in relative, though equal, poverty. The USSR, a militaristic communist state, collapsed primarily due to citizen unrest and poverty, but only to evolve into what some economists refer to as a kleptocracy, or rule through theft. Essentially, after the collapse of the USSR, the country fell into gang rule, until one gang finally took over and now rules in a sort of warlord-like manner. These are, of course, gross simplifications, but essentially what happened.

On the other hand, the United States and a few European countries attempted capitalistic democratic republics. Though this system has endured, it has sort of morphed into a quasi-democratic financial autocracy in many places and has its own problems. Most of which were elucidated in the first chapter. Most notably, there is a huge wealth gap, with less than 3 percent controlling over 95 percent of the wealth. It is a system where a vast number of the population lives hand-to-mouth and month-to-month, where many people are without access to all but the most basic medical care, where our schools have graduating students who can barely read or do basic math, and where people are encouraged to spend more than they can afford and put themselves in debt for life (a kind of wage slavery). Most of the "western" world has adopted some form of this governing system with a few variations and with varying levels of success.

Though there are a myriad of factors, if we boil it down to the simplest of concepts, the difference between the two major systems is the encouragement or discouragement of capitalism.

Now many of you may be saying to yourself, *It's not about capitalism; it's about the freedom and/or liberty of the People,* and ultimately, you'll be correct. But I'd like to propose that both systems in their extreme undermine that—communism, by taking the People's production and making them solely dependent upon the system for their livelihoods, usually involving some sort of forceful military or police compliance, and capitalism through a dog-eat-dog financial system that leaves all but the most ruthless and ambitious, if not just living month-to-month, at least, at the whim of those who have seized and monopolized the industrial and financial (and in some cases prominent in the Central and South Americas military) systems. As well as a systematized process of indebtedness, creating a sort of consensual but involuntary slavery on the part of everyone but the most cautious.

Industry

If we refer back to the beginning and review the three parts of society—government, industry, and the People—we'll see that industry provides the products and services a society wants and needs, creates commerce, innovates, generates wealth and value, and produces the means for society to grow and prosper. Or essentially, it creates the financial well-being of society.

With this in mind, we must go back to that all-important question: do we promote or discourage capitalism? Both systems have their good and bad points. Communism/socialism (in theory) is designed so that everyone has what they need, but the opportunity for growth or wealth building is not available. While capitalism promises unlimited wealth and growth potential, it tends to leave many behind to "fend for themselves." Hopefully, the answer should be pretty obvious, as even the most communistic societies have all eventually adopted some form of capitalistic behavior. But unchecked capitalism has proven to be equally detrimental in the form of concentrated wealth, ecological exploitation, and even actual slavery. But hinder capitalism too much, and things like innovation, motivation, production quality, and general growth stagnate. So some form of regulated and harnessed capitalism needs to be developed. A system where people have the opportunity to make as much money as they can figure out how, while at the same time supporting and creating a stable, secure society for all.

The first limit on capitalism should be a limit on market control.

Historically, antitrust legislation prevented a single entity from controlling or monopolizing any one industry or geographic area, as it was obvious to all that if one group controlled a large enough portion of any industry, it undermined the benefits of open-market competition and potentially placed too much power in one place to control prices and quality. This antitrust legislation was responsible for some of the most historic corporate breakups, such as Standard Oil and AT&T. But in 1999/2000, the attempt to break up Microsoft largely failed. Microsoft CEO Bill Gates successfully argued that Microsoft was dedicated to providing the consumer with the best product at the best price and that splitting up the company would interfere with that mission, and he was able to largely avoid the breakup of his company.

Since then, we've seen a few companies grow to the point where they largely dominate the markets they operate in, namely, Google in the information realm, Walmart in consumer goods stores, and Amazon in online sales and product delivery. Now regardless of how you feel about the products and services you receive from these companies, I use all three regularly, but opportunities to compete with them are very limited. Their control over the market share in their respective industries makes doing business opposite them nearly impossible. This, potentially, places them in a position to manipulate the market and availability of their products and services should their control suddenly be subjected to the "curse of bigness," as described by Justice Douglas:

> The Curse of Bigness shows how size can become
> a menace—both industrial and social. It can
> be an industrial menace because it creates gross
> inequalities against existing or putative compet-
> itors. It can be a social menace...In final anal-
> ysis, size in steel is the measure of the power of
> a handful of men over our economy...The phi-
> losophy of the Sherman Act is that it should not
> exist...Industrial power should be decentralized.

> It should be scattered into many hands so that
> the fortunes of the people will not be dependent
> on the whim or caprice, the political prejudices,
> or the emotional stability of a few self-appointed
> men. (Dissenting view of Justice Douglas, US vs.
> Columbia Steel Co.)

With this in mind, individual companies or organized groups of companies should be limited to some percentage of their respective markets. A good starting place would be 45 percent. This will still allow for the advantages of scale but leave enough market share for small, innovative competitors to compete. The existing anti-trust legislation—the 1890 Sherman Act, the 1914 Federal Trade Commission Act, and the Clayton Acts—were and are excellent foundations for this.

The second limit or responsibility placed on industry should be providing funding for society. What this means is that the national tax liability should be moved away from the People and placed on industry. As referenced earlier, approximately 80 percent of the government's income comes from personal income tax, retirement taxes, and social insurance. This creates an unnecessary burden and pressure on the People. If we move the funding for government around the economic circle to industry, this will be far more efficient, eliminate many problems, and take the burden of direct taxation off the People. The current US GNP is roughly $25T.[12] The government's annual revenue is roughly $5T[13], 80 percent of which comes directly out of the People's pockets through direct taxation. If industry is required to contribute 20 percent of gross revenue back to society in the form of an industry tax, this will solve many issues.

Firstly, bookkeeping. Industry is already doing it. Every business keeps books, and successful businesses keep extensive books. So adding a line item for taxes is a simple issue. Thus removing this task

---

[12]   https://tradingeconomics.com/united-states/gdp
[13]   https://fiscaldata.treasury.gov/americas-finance-guide/

from the taxpayer, who may or may not do much bookkeeping in their lives.

Second, ease of accountability. Since most industries provide regular economic reports to shareholders, owners, and management, tracking tax liability is streamlined as the government simply gets the same economic documents everyone else gets. This will essentially do away with audits and invasive investigations by the taxing agencies in all but the most extreme cases. It also reduces the number of tax returns that must be examined and processed since now only businesses will be reporting instead of every adult individual.

Third, it takes the immediate tax burden off the People. Essentially, the People still pay the tax, but it comes to them through the products and services they buy or use, as Industry will simply pass the burden onto their customers through pricing. But the People won't feel the heavy hand of taxation as the IRS or other tax agency comes to them directly. Employees will see an immediate increase in their take-home pay as withholding will cease, giving individuals more discretionary income. As most middle- or upper-income employees are taxed at a rate somewhere between 20 and 30 percent, these portions of society will see an increase in their buying power. This will also largely remove the fear and apprehension the People have concerning the encroachment of the government into their financial lives. Ultimately creating a calmer and more stable society.

Fourthly, avoiding tax liability through the manipulation of a complex tax code is largely eliminated. As the tax is levied on gross revenue, the majority of tax deductions, shelters, and diversions are eliminated. Much of the motivation for tax avoidance is also eliminated since the cost of the tax is passed onto the consumer through product and service pricing. It would be nice to see some of that cost offset by shareholder profit, but again, humans will be humans.

Fifthly, it is as fair a tax as taxes come. Each person is taxed directly in proportion to their lifestyle, as the taxes are essentially paid through the cost of the products and services each person uses.

Sixthly, it provides a nice medium between the problem of capitalism vs. socialism. It promotes the motivation for someone to make as much as they're able through innovation, quality, hard work, etc., while providing for societal programs and the well-being of everyone.

Additionally, the government and society will actually have a nearly 60 percent increase in usable revenue through this system without any increase in the relative tax burden of the People. Combined with the new budget policy described earlier, and since, according to the Grace Commission, 30 percent of taxes are uncollected and 30 percent are wasted, both of these tax losses can be eliminated. Imagine if that 60 percent were actually made available for the benefit of society. This windfall for the government can be passed onto the lower-income sections of society, who may indeed be negatively affected by the increase in products and services due to the industry tax.

The last restriction that should be placed on industry is a limitation on patents. All patents should expire after ten years. In the current system, patents expire after twenty years. However, there is a practice of repatenting an existing patent, stating some minor changes. This essentially allows a patent to remain in effect indefinitely. We see this most often in the pharmaceutical industry, and it is one of the reasons for outrageously priced medications. Requiring all patents to expire ten years from the time of application, with no exceptions, will have a twofold effect. First, it will limit the amount of time a proprietary advantage may be maintained. It provides enough time for a novel technology to be capitalized upon before becoming public domain, but it also gives everyone the opportunity to use it once it has become public knowledge. Second, it limits the ability to own and suppress competing technologies by those who do not want to compete with innovation. Competition in industry is essential to promoting innovation and advancement in our society as well as preserving fair and competitive options for the society as a whole.

The People

The last part of our new system is, of course, the People themselves. Society is pulled or pushed along by the People who make it up. In general, people everywhere are largely looking for the same things—acceptance, love, a feeling of security in their lives, a feeling of having a place in society, and being respected by others. Some of the things researchers have identified as aspects of a healthy community are a common set of goals, freedom of expression, the addressing of members' concerns, clear policies and obligations, fairness, interaction and communication, and leaders who embody the values of the community. Most people naturally resist change. As mentioned earlier, our founding fathers were very aware of this, as evidenced by actually penning it into the Declaration of Independence:

> "…all experience hath shewn, that mankind are
> more disposed to suffer, while evils are sufferable,
> than to right themselves by abolishing the forms
> to which they are accustomed…

The good news is that the changes needed to bring our society together as a whole are, in this author's opinion, very small. We pretty much all want the same thing, as described above. All it will take is just a little bit of acceptance that everyone has value and offers something to the whole. We don't all have to agree. We don't have to get along. We don't even have to like each other. We just need to accept that everyone has value and recognize that even if the other person is completely different from ourselves, society, as a whole, is diminished without them. The strongest environments are those with the most diverse populations living and cooperating. Charles Darwin put forth the concept of "survival of the fittest" in his groundbreaking work *The Origin of Species.* But this concept falls short of what this author feels is the actual truth. In truth, survival comes to those species who adapt and cooperate the best within their environments and with the other species living alongside them.

It may not always be easy, but it's our differences that make us strong. America was built on the idea of diversity. It's etched in stone on one of our most identifiable icons, the Statue of Liberty.

> …Give me your tired, your poor, your huddled
> masses yearning to breathe free…

Fundamental Personal Rights

There's been a lot of discussion about personal Rights. The Bill of Rights and Declaration of Independence lay down a set of Rights for citizens of the United States. Among these are life, liberty, the pursuit of happiness, free speech, peaceful assembly, freedom of religion, the Right to keep and bear arms in order to maintain a militia, etc. Many countries, as well as the UN, have elucidated a list of human Rights that should be granted to all, which go beyond those set down by our founding fathers.

All these concepts should be taken into consideration. However, when one talks about Rights, what are we really talking about? Some say our Rights are "God-given," or, as the founding fathers wrote, "endowed by their Creator." But if that were the case, wouldn't everyone have them, and we'd be incapable of violating anyone's? Well that's certainly not the case. People's so-called "God-given" Rights are violated every day. Actually, most humans live in environments or societies where these so-called God-given Rights are nothing more than a pipe dream.

So if our Rights aren't God-given, then they must come from somewhere else. In most cases, our Rights are granted and protected by the state. Now that's all well and good as long as the state continues to function in the People's best interest. But the state is, as with all things, run by humans. So if the humans running the state become corrupted, too powerful, or too scared, our Rights can be limited, curtailed, or all together abolished with little more than the stroke of a pen, as we've seen in recent decades. So are they really Rights? It sounds more like a series of privileges that can be taken away for any number of reasons. There's a bumper sticker that says, "Rights are nothing more than limitations on power, agreed to by those in power, in order to stay in power." That's interesting, and there may actually be some truth there.

So what do we do about the question of Rights? First, the Law must allow for redress of the things we, as a society, deem to be important. Second, but most importantly, society as a whole must agree that certain behaviors are unacceptable. Rights, if there is such a thing, have to come directly from society. Directly from each other. Rights must apply to everyone, regardless of race, creed, gender, country of origin, or any other factor. *Rights must apply to everyone.* I'm not going to presume to dictate what those Rights are or even should be. I'll leave that to the rest of you to decide for yourselves. But unlike citizenship, Rights need to be granted and are inviolable for EVERYONE.

An idea concerning what Rights an individual has or can express might be: An individual has the right to do anything they wish to the extent of the Law. Imagine an area defined by a set of rules (the Law). Inside this area, a person is allowed to do anything they like until they bump into one of the defining boundaries of the Law. If the line isn't crossed, no problem, no harm, no foul. But cross the line, and the consequences are quick and severe. You can think of it as a free zone bounded by a set of despotic rules. Stay within the zone (behavior) dictated by the edges (the Law), and all is good. Cross the line, and the hammer comes down.

If the Law (as described above) is broad enough and easily understood, then the question of Rights becomes moot.

Atrocities of the Past

Most societies today have been built on the backs of, and are currently made up of, numerous cultural groups. Many of these have been abused or mistreated along the journey to the present day. We must recognize the pain and sacrifice suffered by those people. Since no recompense can be made to the individuals who suffered those injustices, we should honor their sacrifice and give thanks for the lessons we've learned from them in hopes that such atrocities never happen again. By evolving society into a more modern, prosperous, safe, and respectful environment for all humans, we can make their sacrifices mean something. A holiday commemorating their sacrifice should be established.

Conclusion

Humans and, especially, human society are very complex. Human society and our social structure are unique on this planet. No other organism or group of organisms operates in such large and complex groups as humans. It's a uniquely human trait. The fact that humans can operate together in groups of thousands and maintain complex and unique individual relationships is truly a wonder. Coupled with the fact that everyone is, at least initially, essentially out for themselves, the whole thing is mind-boggling.

Trying to manage this seems like an insurmountable task, but it's that task that seems to make it possible. Many people have contributed to this quest, and improvements and growth have been constant throughout human history.

It is this author's opinion that, for the most part, basic society runs pretty well on its own. Life at the lowest and most basic levels of society usually changes very little through the turmoil and changes of government policies and leaders. This, of course, doesn't apply to primitive societies, where violence over territory or ideology is the ruling norm. In these primitive societies, all but the strongest and most violent suffer. But the ideas presented here are not meant for primitives. They're meant for relatively civilized societies. There is definitely a need for some hard boundaries concerning the curtailment of our basic human nature to do for ourselves, and limited, qualified leadership is definitely a good thing. But it has been my experience that simplicity tends to build stronger, more reliable systems. Human society is a chaotic and messy thing, but that is sort of the beauty of it. Let it be what it is. Allow society to do what it does, limit the extremes of power and action, and let the rest essentially take care of itself. In this, I believe human society can bloom into something beautiful beyond our imaginations.

Therefore, I humbly submit the above observations and suggestions as additions to the grand experiment of human societal management and hope these suggestions prove helpful in promoting the growth and development of human society into the future.

Your feedback is very valuable to me. Please scan here to leave a review. Thank you.

Rob Pendell

Glossary

Person (people). Any human beyond ninety days from conception, or anything, terrestrial or otherwise, which has the sentience and intelligence to claim its Rights under the Law.

Basic bedding. Anything a person can completely separate themselves from the ground; no less than two inches in thickness; one wool blanket free from holes; no less than twenty-four square feet per person.

Basic shelter. Any enclosed space that separates a person from the elements and maintains an internal temperature between 60 and 85 degrees Fahrenheit; one functional toilet and one sink with running water for every ten persons. All persons must vacate the shelter with all their belongings between the hours of 9:00 a.m. and 4:00 p.m. in order that the facility may be cleaned (unless the weather poses an imminent threat to life or limb).

Basic subsistence. It consists of 1,200 calories for persons under the age of ten per day, 2,000 calories for persons over the age of ten per day, and one gallon of potable water per person per day.

Emergency life-saving medical care. Medical care to prevent imminent death due to an accident.

About the Author

Rob Pendell is a Nomad scholar and has been referred to as a "renaissance man." He is an author, artist, musician, business entrepreneur, world traveler, veteran, graduate, inmate, farmer, educator, adventurer, outlaw, smuggler, political advocate, black belt, and that guy living in a van down by the river. Rob's wide breadth of experience has given him a unique perspective on the world and society. Through his many careers, he has witnessed our "system" from both the inside and out. Combining his experience and understanding of basic human nature, he strives to promote living your best life and creating the healthiest society possible.